Date: 05/22/12

SP J 394.262 BRO
Brode, Robyn.
May /

May/Mayo

By/Por Robyn Brode

Reading Consultant/Consultora de lectura: Linda Cornwell,
Literacy Connections Consulting/consultora de lectoescritura

WEEKLY READER®
PUBLISHING

Please visit our web site at **www.garethstevens.com**.
For a free catalog describing our list of high-quality books, call 1-800-542-2595 (USA)
or 1-800-387-3178 (Canada). Our fax: 1-877-542-2596

Library of Congress Cataloging-in-Publication Data

    [May. Spanish & English]
    May / by Robyn Brode ; reading consultant, Linda Cornwell — Mayo / por Robyn Brode ;
    consultora de lectura, Linda Cornwell.
        p. cm. — (Months of the year — Meses del año)
    English and Spanish in parallel text.
    Includes bibliographical references and index.
    ISBN-10: 1-4339-1933-8   ISBN-13: 978-1-4339-1933-6 (lib. bdg.)
    ISBN-10: 1-4339-2110-3   ISBN-13: 978-1-4339-2110-0 (softcover)
    1. May (Month)—Juvenile literature.   2. Holidays—United States—Juvenile literature.
    3. Spring—United States—Juvenile literature. I. Cornwell, Linda. II. Title.
    GT4803.B7693   2010b
    394.262—dc22   2009013363

This edition first published in 2010 by
Weekly Reader® Books
An Imprint of Gareth Stevens Publishing
1 Reader's Digest Road
Pleasantville, NY 10570-7000 USA

Executive Managing Editor: Lisa M. Herrington
Senior Editors: Barbara Bakowski, Jennifer Magid-Schiller
Designer: Jennifer Ryder-Talbot
Translators: Tatiana Acosta and Guillermo Gutiérrez

Photo Credits: Cover, back cover, title, pp. 7, 19, 21 © Ariel Skelley/Weekly Reader; p. 9 © Masterfile;
p. 11 © David P. Smith/Shutterstock; p. 13 © iofoto/Shutterstock; p. 15 © Photodisc/SuperStock; p. 17
© artcphotos/Shutterstock

Printed in the United States of America

1 2 3 4 5 6 7 8 9 10 11 10 09

Table of Contents/Contenido

Boldface words appear in the glossary.
- - - - - - - -
Las palabras en **negrita** aparecen en el glosario.

Welcome to May!

May is the fifth month of the year.

May has 31 days.

- - - - - - - - - -

¡Bienvenidos a mayo!

Mayo es el quinto mes del año.

Mayo tiene 31 días.

Months of the Year/Meses del año

Month/Mes	Number of Days/Días en el mes
1 January/Enero	31
2 February/Febrero	28 or 29*/28 ó 29*
3 March/Marzo	31
4 April/Abril	30
5 **May/Mayo**	**31**
6 June/Junio	30
7 July/Julio	31
8 August/Agosto	31
9 September/Septiembre	30
10 October/Octubre	31
11 November/Noviembre	30
12 December/Diciembre	31

*February has an extra day every fourth year./Febrero tiene un día extra cada cuatro años.

Spring Weather

May is a **spring** month. In many places, flowers grow. People care for their gardens.

- - - - - - - - - -

Tiempo de primavera

Mayo es uno de los meses de **primavera**. En muchos lugares, comienzan a salir las flores. La gente trabaja en su jardín.

It is warm outside. Kids go to the playground or the park to play.

— — — — — — — — —

Hace buen tiempo. Los niños van a jugar al parque.

Special Days

Cinco de Mayo is Spanish for "the fifth of May." On May 5, people celebrate Mexican **culture** with special foods, music, and dancing.

- - - - - - - - -

Días especiales

El **Cinco de Mayo** celebramos la **cultura** mexicana con comidas, música y bailes especiales.

enchilada

The second Sunday in May is Mother's Day. Kids give their mothers cards and gifts. People tell their moms how much they are loved.

— — — — — — — — — —

El segundo domingo de mayo es el Día de la Madre. Los niños entregan tarjetas y regalos a su madre. La gente le dice a su mamá lo mucho que la quiere.

On Mother's Day, some kids give cards to their grandmothers and other women who are special, too.

— — — — — — — —

El Día de la Madre, algunos niños también dan tarjetas a sus abuelas y a otras mujeres importantes en su vida.

 Who will get a card from you on Mother's Day?
— — — — — — — —
¿A quién darás una tarjeta el Día de la Madre?

Memorial Day is the last Monday in May. This holiday honors Americans who lost their lives in wars. On this day, many people hang our country's flag.

— — — — — — — — —

El último lunes de mayo es **Memorial Day** (Día de los Caídos). En esta fiesta se honra a los estadounidenses que perdieron la vida en una guerra. Ese día, muchas personas cuelgan la bandera de nuestro país.

School Is Out!

In some places, school ends in May. In other places, school ends in June.

— — — — — — — — —

¡Se acabaron las clases!

Hay sitios donde el año escolar acaba en mayo. En otros, las clases terminan en junio.

When does your school year end?
— — — — — — — —
¿Cuándo acaba tu año escolar?

When May ends, it is time for June to begin. Soon it will be time for summer **vacation**!

- - - - - - - - - -

Cuando mayo termina, empieza junio. ¡Pronto llegarán las **vacaciones** de verano!

Glossary/Glosario

Cinco de Mayo: May 5, a special day when people celebrate Mexican culture

culture: the beliefs and customs that make up the way of life of a group of people

Memorial Day: a holiday that honors Americans who lost their lives in wars

spring: the season between winter and summer, when the air warms and flowers and plants begin to grow

vacation: time away from school or work

-- -- -- -- -- -- -- -- --

Cinco de Mayo: día especial en que se celebra la cultura mexicana

cultura: creencias y costumbres que forman el modo de vida de un grupo de personas

Memorial Day: fiesta en la que se honra a los estadounidenses que perdieron la vida en una guerra

primavera: la estación del año entre el invierno y el verano. En primavera, el aire se hace más caliente y las flores y las plantas empiezan a crecer.

vacaciones: periodo de descanso de las actividades de la escuela o del trabajo

22

For More Information/Más información

Books/Libros

Celebrate! It's Cinco de Mayo!/¡Celebremos! ¡Es el Cinco de Mayo!
Janice Levy (Albert Whitman and Company, 2007)

Memorial Day/Día de los Caídos. Our Country's Holidays/
Las fiestas de nuestra nación (series). Sheri Dean (Gareth Stevens
Publishing, 2006)

Web Sites/Páginas web

Cinco de Mayo
www.theholidayzone.com/cinco/cinco-de-mayo-songs.html
Learn fun songs for Cinco de Mayo./Aprendan canciones divertidas
para el Cinco de Mayo.

Memorial Day/*Memorial Day* (Día de los Caídos)
www.apples4theteacher.com/holidays/memorial-day
Find crafts, activities, and Memorial Day poems./Encuentren
manualidades, actividades y poemas relacionados con
Memorial Day.

Publisher's note to educators and parents: Our editors have carefully reviewed these web sites to ensure that they are suitable for children. Many web sites change frequently, however, and we cannot guarantee that a site's future contents will continue to meet our high standards of quality and educational value. Be advised that children should be closely supervised whenever they access the Internet.

Nota de la editorial a los padres y educadores: Nuestros editores han revisado con cuidado las páginas web para asegurarse de que son apropiadas para niños. Sin embargo, muchas páginas web cambian con frecuencia, y no podemos garantizar que sus contenidos futuros sigan conservando nuestros elevados estándares de calidad y de interés educativo. Tengan en cuenta que los niños deben ser supervisados atentamente siempre que accedan a Internet.

Index/Índice

About the Author

Robyn Brode has been a teacher, a writer, and an editor in the book publishing field for many years. She earned a bachelor's degree in English literature from the University of California, Berkeley.

- - - - - - - -

Información sobre la autora

Robyn Brode ha sido maestra, escritora y editora de libros durante muchos años. Obtuvo su licenciatura en literatura inglesa en la Universidad de California, Berkeley.